Love

by Iain Gray

WRITING *to* REMEMBER

79 Main Street, Newtongrange,
Midlothian EH22 4NA
Tel: 0131 344 0414   Fax: 0845 075 6085
E-mail: info@lang-syne.co.uk
www.langsyneshop.co.uk

Design by Dorothy Meikle
Printed by Printwell Ltd
© Lang Syne Publishers Ltd 2021

All rights reserved. No part of this publication may be reproduced, stored or introduced into a retrieval system, or transmitted in any form or by any means (electronic, mechanical, photocopying, recording or otherwise) without the prior written permission of Lang Syne Publishers Ltd.

ISBN 978-1-85217-787-4

Love

MOTTO:
None recorded

CREST:
A bird against the background of a cross

TERRITORIES include:
Cambridgeshire, Oxfordshire,
Kent, Norfolk

NAME variations include:
Luf
Lufe
Luff

Chapter one:

The origins of popular surnames

by George Forbes and Iain Gray

***If you don't know where you came from, you won't know where you're going** is a frequently quoted observation and one that has a particular resonance today when there has been a marked upsurge in interest in genealogy, with increasing numbers of people curious to trace their family roots.*

Main sources for genealogical research include census returns and official records of births, marriages and deaths – and the key to unlocking the detail they contain is obviously a family surname, one that has been 'inherited' and passed from generation to generation.

No matter our station in life, we all have a surname – but it was not until about the middle of the fourteenth century that the practice of being identified by a particular surname became commonly established throughout the British Isles.

Previous to this, it was normal for a person to be identified through the use of only a forename.

But as population gradually increased and there were many more people with the same forename, surnames were adopted to distinguish one person, or community, from another.

Many common English surnames are patronymic in origin, meaning they stem from the forename of one's father – with 'Johnson,' for example, indicating 'son of John.'

It was the Normans, in the wake of their eleventh century conquest of Anglo-Saxon England, a pivotal moment in the nation's history, who first brought surnames into usage – although it was a gradual process.

For the Normans, these were names initially based on the title of their estates, local villages and chateaux in France to distinguish and identify these landholdings.

Such grand descriptions also helped enhance the prestige of these warlords and generally glorify their lofty positions high above the humble serfs slaving away below in the pecking order who had only single names, often with Biblical connotations as in Pierre and Jacques.

The only descriptive distinctions among the peasantry concerned their occupations, like 'Pierre the swineherd' or 'Jacques the ferryman.'

Roots of surnames that came into usage in England not only included Norman-French, but also Old French, Old Norse, Old English, Middle English, German, Latin, Greek, Hebrew and the Gaelic languages of the Celts.

The Normans themselves were originally Vikings, or 'Northmen', who raided, colonised and eventually settled down around the French coastline.

They had sailed up the Seine in their longboats in 900AD under their ferocious leader Rollo and ruled the roost in north eastern France before sailing over to conquer England in 1066 under Duke William of Normandy – better known to posterity as William the Conqueror, or King William I of England.

Granted lands in the newly-conquered England, some of their descendants later acquired territories in Wales, Scotland and Ireland – taking not only their own surnames, but also the practice of adopting a surname, with them.

But it was in England where Norman rule and custom first impacted, particularly in relation to the adoption of surnames.

This is reflected in the famous *Domesday Book*, a massive survey of much of England and Wales, ordered by William I, to determine who owned what, what it was worth and therefore how much they were liable to pay in taxes to the voracious Royal Exchequer.

Completed in 1086 and now held in the National Archives in Kew, London, 'Domesday' was an Old English word meaning 'Day of Judgement.'

This was because, in the words of one contemporary chronicler, "its decisions, like those of the Last Judgement, are unalterable."

It had been a requirement of all those English landholders – from the richest to the poorest – that they identify themselves for the purposes of the survey and for future reference by means of a surname.

This is why the *Domesday Book*, although written in Latin as was the practice for several centuries with both civic and ecclesiastical records, is an invaluable source for the early appearance of a wide range of English surnames.

Several of these names were coined in connection with occupations.

These include Baker and Smith, while Cooks, Chamberlains, Constables and Porters were to be found carrying out duties in large medieval households.

The church's influence can be found in names such as Bishop, Friar and Monk while the popular name of Bennett derives from the late fifth to mid-sixth century Saint Benedict, founder of the Benedictine order of monks.

The early medical profession is represented by Barber, while businessmen produced names that include Merchant and Sellers.

Down at the village watermill, the names that cropped up included Millar/Miller, Walker and Fuller, while other self-explanatory trades included Cooper, Tailor, Mason and Wright.

Even the scenery was utilised as in Moor, Hill, Wood and Forrest – while the hunt and the chase supplied names that include Hunter, Falconer, Fowler and Fox.

Colours are also a source of popular surnames, as in Black, Brown, Gray/Grey, Green and White, and would have denoted the colour of the clothing the person habitually wore or, apart from the obvious exception of 'Green', one's hair colouring or even complexion.

The surname Red developed into Reid, while

Love 9

Blue was rare and no-one wanted to be associated with yellow.

Rather self-important individuals took surnames that include Goodman and Wiseman, while physical attributes crept into surnames such as Small and Little.

Many families proudly boast the heraldic device known as a Coat of Arms, as featured on our front cover.

The central motif of the Coat of Arms would originally have been what was borne on the shield of a warrior to distinguish himself from others on the battlefield.

Not featured on the Coat of Arms, but highlighted on page three, is the family motto and related crest – with the latter frequently different from the central motif.

Adding further variety to the rich cultural heritage that is represented by surnames is the appearance in recent times in lists of the 100 most common names found in England of ones that include Khan, Patel and Singh – names that have proud roots in the vast sub-continent of India.

Echoes of a far distant past can still be found in our surnames and they can be borne with pride in commemoration of our forebears.

Chapter two:

Piracy and politics

A name of ancient roots, 'Love' has two possible points of origin of which the most commonly accepted is that it derives from the French 'loup' or 'lo(u)ve', indicating 'wolf' and which became popular as a surname in the wake of the Norman Conquest of 1066.

Another possible source, meanwhile, is from the decidedly less ferocious Anglo-Saxon, or Old English, 'lufu', meaning 'love' as in endearment.

By whatever means it came to be adopted as a surname, it became particularly prevalent from earliest times in Cambridgeshire, Oxfordshire, Kent and Norfolk – but not exclusively confined to these present-day English counties.

In common with many family names, there are a number of Love Coats of Arms – the most common of which feature a bird against the background of a cross as the crest – but no mottoes have been recorded.

In 1424 the death of a Nicholas Love, also known as Nicholas Luff, is recorded in Yorkshire, where he was the first prior of a Carthusian religious house at Mount Grace.

Although his date of birth is not known, facts that do relate to his life and times, including his duties as a prior, reveal he was also responsible for the translation of the popular Franciscan meditational manual *Meditations on the Life of Christ* from French into English as *The Mirror of the Blessed Life of Jesus Christ*.

On a decidedly less spiritual level, Peter Love was the late sixteenth century English pirate who forged an unholy alliance with a Scottish outlaw.

His date of birth is not known, but he is understood to have born in Lewes, now the county town of East Sussex.

Assembling a cut-throat crew and as captain of the pirate ship *Priam*, he terrorised the shipping lanes by swooping on unsuspecting vessels and plundering their cargo.

At an indeterminate date between about 1598 and 1610 he narrowly escaped capture off the Irish coast and fled northwards to the Outer Hebrides, anchoring near Bernera within Loch Roag, Isle of Lewis.

The *Priam* was crammed with a valuable

booty of silver plate, hides, sugar, cochineal, ginger, pepper and cinnamon looted from an English ship and a chest of precious jewels and a substantial number of muskets from a Dutch vessel.

But the pirates and their ill-gotten gains were at the mercy of an outlaw who had established a base on a rock stack on the small island of Bearasaigh, within the loch.

Fortunately, however, this was at an opportune time for both Love and the outlaw Neil MacLeod, son of the late chief of the MacLeods of Lewis.

This was during the reign of King James VI (future James I of England), when an Act of Parliament was passed in 1597 to suppress what was considered to be the 'barbarous inhumanity' of Highlanders and Islanders such as the MacLeods of Lewis.

The monarch, certainly no friend of his far-flung western seaboard and northern subjects, accordingly issued what were known as *Letters of Fire and Sword* to bring the unruly clansmen to heel.

In what became known as the Daunting of the Isles, Lewis was singled out for special attention in a campaign that would today be described as a form of ethnic cleansing.

Seeking to justify the savage attack to be

launched on the islanders, the Scottish Privy Council condemned 'the beastly and monstrous cruelties' that they inflicted upon one another, and pointed out that the rich and fertile lands of Lewis would be better managed by others.

Accordingly, in 1598, the king issued a charter, or contract, to a band of speculators who became known as the Fife Adventurers.

Backed by a 600-strong force of mercenaries led by the Duke of Lennox, the adventurers attempted to wipe out the inhabitants of Lewis and take their lands for themselves.

They received a rude shock, however, when the hardy band of natives fought back with such ferocity that the adventurers were forced to withdraw; another force was later sent to renew the attempt at bringing the clansmen to heel, but this also proved abortive.

This is why Neil MacLeod was to be found perched above a near-impregnable rock stack when Love dropped anchor in Loch Roag – and the pair quickly realised the benefit of combining their resources.

Using Lewis as his base, Love and his crew captured a number of ships and their cargo, including one owned by Thomas Fleming, of the Scottish east coast village of Anstruther.

Fleming was taken prisoner, while a number of crew from a captured Flemish ship were taken to work as slaves on Lewis.

As Love and MacLeod gleefully shared their loot among themselves and their men, the bond between them is reputed to have become so close that even a marriage was mooted between the pirate captain and a kinsman of the clansman.

But self-interest and greed eventually overcame any loyalty which may have existed between the pair and MacLeod attempted to seize the unsuspecting pirates during a lavish and drunken feast he had organised.

A vicious struggle ensued, with a number of pirates killed and both Love and the *Priam* seized.

Hoping to curry favour with the authorities, MacLeod sent a message to the Privy Council in Edinburgh informing them of Love's capture, while a substantial sum of money found on the *Priam* was divided up among MacLeod and his followers – something he decided not to divulge to the council.

The hapless Love and nine of his men were handed over and, tried in Edinburgh on December 8,

1610, found guilty of piracy and condemned to be hanged.

Translated from Old Scots, their sentence read that they should "be taken to a gibbet upon the sands of Leith, within the flood-mark, and there be hanged until they be dead."

But MacLeod's bid to ingratiate himself with the authorities and receive a reprieve for his own crimes failed, and he was forced to flee his Lewis sanctuary in early 1613 and seek refuge on the Isle of Harris with his kinsman Rory Mor MacLeod of Harris and Dunvegan.

Rory promised to take him to London in hope of obtaining a pardon for his previous rebellion – but he betrayed his kinsman by turning him over to the authorities when they reached Glasgow.

Put on trial and found guilty of high treason, he met the same fate as his erstwhile partner in crime the pirate Peter Love, while his son was banished to England.

Another infamous seventeenth century bearer of the Love name was the English lawyer and politician Nicholas Love, one of the regicides – responsible for the death of a monarch – of King Charles I.

Born in 1608 and elected MP (Member of

Parliament) for Winchester in 1645, he was one of the judges at the king's trial for high treason before Parliament in January of 1649.

This was following the First English Civil War of 1642 to 1646 that had been sparked off by Charles' claim to the Divine Right of Kings and supremacy over Parliament.

Found guilty, he was beheaded outside the Palace of Whitehall on January 30, while England's 'Lord Protector' Oliver Cromwell consolidated his hold over Parliament and the nation, backed up by the swords and muskets of the New Model Army.

Following the restoration of the monarchy in 1660 under King Charles II, many of those who had presided at his father's trial were marked men.

While some were pardoned, others such as Nicholas Love were forced to flee into exile – in his case to Switzerland, where he died in 1682.

Those who did not escape were put on trial and six executed – but nor did leading regicides who had already died, such as Cromwell, who had shuffled off this mortal coil in 1658, escape punishment.

Buried at Westminster Abbey, his body was disinterred and ignominiously hanged, drawn and quartered in a grisly posthumous execution.

Chapter three:

Honours and distinction

On the battlefields of nineteenth century Europe, Sir James Frederick Love was the distinguished British Army officer who fought at both the battles of Corunna and Waterloo during the Napoleonic Wars of 1803 to 1815.

Born in 1789, he was commissioned into the 52nd Regiment of Foot in 1804 and was present in Spain during the Peninsular War of 1808 to 1814, part of the wider Napoleonic Wars.

By January of 1809 Napoleon had defeated the Spanish army, and their allies the British were forced to withdraw to the port of Corunna on the northern coast of Galicia.

Arriving exhausted at the port, having been harried all along the way by the French, they found the ships to evacuate them were not yet there and, much in the manner of Dunkirk just over 130 years later, had to fight a desperate rear guard action to embark to safety once the vessels did arrive.

It was also during this battle, known to the Spanish as the battle of Elvina, that the British commander Sir John Moore was killed – immortalised in the famous 1817 poem by Charles Wolfe *The Burial of Sir John Moore after Corunna*.

Also present at the battle of Waterloo, in Belgium, on June 18, 1815, when a British army under the command of the Duke of Wellington and allies including the Prussians famously defeated Napoleon, Sir Frederick Love later served in posts including Lieutenant Governor of Jersey and, appointed in 1857, Inspector-General of Infantry.

He died in 1866, two years after being promoted to the rank of general and the recipient of honours and awards including Knight Grand Cross of the Order of the Bath.

In the twentieth century and in a different arena of combat, Hannah Lincoln Harkness, better known as Nancy and by her married name Nancy Harkness Love, was the pioneering American aviator born in 1914 in Houghton, Michigan.

Fascinated with flight from an early age, she was aged only 16 when she took her first lesson, earning her pilot's license within less than a month.

Coming to national attention in 1932 when she gained a commercial license while studying at college in New York, she earned money by taking fellow students on flights aboard aircraft she rented from a local airport.

Along with her husband Robert M. Love, the Air Corps Reserve major whom she married in 1936, she ran the Boston-based company Inter City Aviation, while also competing in a number of national air races – meantime, with her prowess in the air commanding increasing attention, she was entrusted as a test pilot for a civilian aeroplane manufacturer.

With America's entry into the Second World War following the Japanese bombing of Pearl Harbor in December of 1942, there was a need for skilled pilots to ferry military aircraft from factories to air bases and Love fulfilled this need as commander of the Women Airforce Service Pilots group (WASP).

These female pilots flew almost every type of USAAF (United States Army Air Force) aeroplane, with Love the first woman to pilot the Boeing B-17 Flying Fortress Bomber and the P-51 Mustang fighter.

At the end of the war she and her husband, who had served as deputy chief of staff of Ferrying Command, were both decorated at the same ceremony.

While her husband received the Distinguished Service Medal, she was the recipient of the Air Medal for her "operational leadership in the successful training and assignment of over 300 qualified women fliers in the flying of advanced military aircraft."

Given the rank of lieutenant colonel in the U.S. Air Force Reserve following the creation after the war of the USAF (United States Air Force), she died in 1976 while posthumous honours include induction into the National Aviation Hall of Fame and the Michigan Women's Hall of Fame.

From the heights of the heavens to the depths of the ground, Iris Cornelia Love, born in New York in 1933 and better known as Iris C. Love, was the American classical archaeologist famed for her discovery of the fabled Temple of Aphrodite.

Her mother Audrey Josephthal was a great-great granddaughter of the immensely wealthy entrepreneur Meyer Guggenheim and she and her husband Cornelius Love and their friends encouraged her interest from an early age in art history and archaeology.

These influential friends included the archaeologist Gisela Richter and James Rorimer, director of New York's Metropolitan Museum of Art, and Love followed in their footsteps by studying both subjects at institutions including the University of Florence.

While studying in Florence in 1960, she compared Etruscan warrior figures at the city's National Archaeological Museum with ones held by the Metropole.

Discovering that those at the latter were fake, out of respect for her friends associated with the New York museum, she warned its authorities before releasing her findings in publication form.

But the museum responded by making an announcement of the fakes themselves to the *New York Times* – without acknowledging her work.

However, full credit for her expertise came her way in 1969 through the discovery of the remains of the Temple of Aphrodite in what had been the ancient Greek city of Knidos, now in modern-day Turkey.

Having carefully excavated the site, with the cooperation of Turkish archaeologist Aşkidil Akarca, she uncovered what had been the sanctuary dedicated to Aphrodite, known as *Aphrodite Euploia*, or *Aphrodite of the Fair Voyage*, in recognition of one of her aspects as a sea goddess.

Once a popular place of pilgrimage, particularly for seafarers, it had featured a circular Doric column surrounded by colonnades and a statue of the goddess, depicted naked, sculpted by Praxiteles of Athens in 365BC.

The discovery attracted international attention, drawing celebrity visitors including Mick Jagger of the Rolling Stones and his then wife Bianca Jagger – leading to criticism, unfairly levelled at Love, that she had been responsible for 'converting the excavation into an exclusive holiday destination'.

Only the marble base of the statue and fragments of the goddess – not including the head had been unearthed, and further controversy was sparked when Love claimed she had located the original head of Aphrodite in the storage rooms of the British Museum, London.

The claim was hotly disputed by Bernard Ashmole, the museum's curator of Greco-Roman artefacts, stirring an international debate in the media and worlds of academia.

Shrugging off the criticism, Love returned to the search for further shrines to Aphrodite before finally retiring from the field.

She died in April of 2020 – one of the many thousands of victims worldwide of Covid-19.

She had meanwhile devoted her retirement to breeding prize winning dachshunds, while she had

Love 23

also lived for many years with her partner the American gossip columnist Mary Elizabeth Smith.

Born in 1923 and known as 'The Grand Dame of Dish' and at one stage the highest paid print journalist in the United States, Smith penned acerbic columns for *The Washington Post*, *New York Daily News* and *Cosmopolitan* magazine.

Also having worked for the Fox Broadcasting Company, she predeceased her partner by three years.

On a tragic note, the American student and women's lacrosse player Yeardley Love is the inspiration for the One Love Foundation – established by her family to raise awareness about domestic violence, especially relationship violence, following her murder at the hands of a former boyfriend.

Born in 1987 in Baltimore, Maryland, she had been a student at the University of Virginia, in Charlottesville and a member of its lacrosse team when she was murdered by fellow student and lacrosse player George Wesley Huguely V.

Born in 1987 in Washington, D.C., he had been in a relationship with Love for about two years before she ended it because of his aggressive behaviour towards her, usually fuelled by alcohol.

Unable to take the rejection, he began to send

her threatening text messages and emails, and matters came to a violent head on the evening of May 3, 2010 when he gained entry to her apartment near the university.

After kicking down her bedroom door he seized and shook her violently, her head banging repeatedly off the wall, before leaving the apartment and taking items including laptop computers and a notebook.

Huguely was arrested, charged and indicted by a grand jury in April of the following year on first degree and felony murder charges and at his trial the jury returned a verdict of guilty of second degree murder and grand larceny.

On August 20, 2012, he was formally sentenced to 23 years imprisonment, with sentences of 23 years for the second degree murder conviction and one year for the grand larceny conviction to run concurrently.

It was within months of Yeardley Love's murder that her family established the One Love Foundation while, with her having worn jersey No. 1 while playing lacrosse, the team retired the number.

Chapter four:

On the world stage

A co-founder of American band the Beach Boys, Mike Love is the singer and songwriter born in Los Angeles in 1941.

Formed in 1961, the original band line-up was Love, his cousins the brothers Brian, Dennis and Carl Wilson and their friend Al Jardine.

Famed for their California 'surfing sound', hits enjoyed by them and co-written by Love and Brian Wilson include the 1964 *Fun, Fun, Fun*, the 1965 *California Girls* and, from 1966, the classic *Good Vibrations*.

With Bruce Johnston replacing Carl Wilson following his death in 1998 and Love also pursuing a successful solo career, the band is an inductee of the Rock and Roll Hall of Fame.

It was not until the 1990s, meanwhile, after successfully suing for credits on 35 songs, that many of his writing contributions were officially recognised.

He remains uncredited, however, for another 44 he claims to have co-written.

In 1988, following the death of Carl Wilson,

he obtained the exclusive license, along with Bruce Johnston, to tour as the Beach Boys, while other surviving members of the band including Brian Wilson now pursue solo careers.

In the soul music genre, **Airron Love**, born in Philadelphia in 1949, is the singer who in 1968, along with Russell Thompkins, Jr., James Dunn, Herb Morrell and James Smith, formed the top-selling band The Stylistics.

Inducted into the Vocal Group Hall of Fame in 2004, hits recorded by the band throughout the 1970s include *You Make Me Feel Brand New*, *You Are Everything* and *I'm Stone in Love with You*.

Named in 2020 as "one of the most influential singers in alternative culture of the last 30 years", Courtney Michelle Harrison is the American singer, songwriter and actress better known as **Courtney Love**.

Born in San Francisco in 1964, as a leading figure in the genres of punk and grunge she first rose to prominence as vocalist of the alternative rock band Hole, formed in 1989 and with albums that include the 1994 *Live Through This* and, from 1998, *Celebrity Skin*, which was nominated for three Grammy Awards.

Married from 1992 until his death from

self-inflicted gunshot wounds to Kurt Cobain of the band Nirvana, she has also suffered from a number of drug-related problems that led to her receiving a mandatory rehabilitation sentence in 2005.

As an actress, films she has starred in include the 1999 *Man on the Moon* and, from 2002, *Trapped*, while her memoir *Dirty Blonde: The Diaries of Courtney Love*, was published in 2006.

Ranked at No. 84 in *Rolling Stone* magazine's list of 100 Greatest Singers, Darlene Wright is the American singer and actress better known by her stage name **Darlene Love**.

Born in Los Angeles in 1941, as a vocalist she features on recordings by many artistes that include Frank Sinatra's version of *That's Life*, the Ronnettes' *Baby, I Love You*, the Crystals' *Da Doo Ron Ron* and, from 1987, on Irish band U2's remake of *Christmas (Baby Please Come Home)*.

With solo albums including *Introducing Darlene Love*, winner in 1995 of the Rhythm and Blues Foundation's Pioneer Award and an inductee of the Rock and Roll Hall of Fame, as an actress she is known for her role of Trish Murtaugh, the wife of actor Danny Glover's character in the *Lethal Weapon* series of films.

Born in New Orleans in 1982, Richard Preston Butler is the American singer, songwriter, rapper and producer better known by his stage name **Rico Love**.

A writer and producer of hits by solo artist Usher, that include *Throwback* from his 2004 album, in his own right albums include the 2015 *TTLO* and, from 2018, *Even Kings Die*.

In a much different musical genre, **Shirley Love** is the American operatic mezzo-soprano born in Detroit in 1940.

Making her professional debut in 1963 at the Metropolitan Opera, New York, in Mozart's *The Magic Flute*, other noted performances include as The Priestess in *Aida*, Gertrud in *Hänsel und Gretel* and Maddalena in *Rigoletto*.

Bearers of the Love name have also excelled in the highly competitive world of sport.

The younger brother of Mike Love of Beach Boys fame, **Stanley S. Love** is the retired basketball player born in Los Angeles in 1949.

Having played with teams including Oregon Ducks, Baltimore Bullets, Los Angeles Lakers and San Antonio Spurs and an inductee of the University of Oregon Athletics Hall of Fame, he is the father of the basketball player **Kevin Love**. Born in Santa Monica in 1988 and having played for teams including the Cleveland Cavaliers, he was a member of the United States gold medal-winning team at the 2012 Olympics.

On British shores and on the football pitch, **Joanne Love** is the Scottish international midfielder born in 1985 in Paisley.

The holder of more than 75 caps for Scotland, teams she has played for include, in England, Doncaster Rovers Belles, the Cocoa Expos in the United States and, in her native land, Celtic and Glasgow City.

Back on American shores and on the golf course, **Davis Milton Love III** is the player with more than 21 PGA (Professional Golf Association) wins that include the 1997 PGA Championship.

Born in 1964 in Charlotte, North Carolina, he was inducted into the World Golf Hall of Fame in 2017.

From the golf course to the motor racing circuit, **John Love** was the driver born in 1924 in Bulawayo, in what was then Rhodesia, now Zimbabwe.

Having participated in ten Formula One

World Championship Grands Prix, winner of the South African Formula One Championship six times in succession from 1964 to 1969 and winner six times of the Rhodesian Grand Prix, he died in 2005.

On the stage, **Gary Love** is the British actor and director known for his role of Sergeant Tony Wilton in the series *Soldier Soldier*.

Born in 1964 in Kensington, London and with other television acting credits including *Grange Hill*, as a director he has worked on episodes of series including *Waking the Dead*, *Casualty* and *London's Burning*.

Born in 1969 and married for a time to the *EastEnders* television soap actress Patsy Palmer, **Nick Love** is the English film writer and director whose credits include the 2001 *Goodbye Charlie Bright*, the 2004 *The Football Factory* and the 2009 remake of the football hooliganism drama *The Firm*.

Also producer of the 2007 film *Outlaw*, his 2012 *The Sweeney* is based on the British television police drama of the name.

From the stage to the highly cerebral world of mathematics, Augustus Edward Hough Love was the British mathematician better known as **A.E.H. Love**.

Born in 1863 and noted for his work on elasticity and wave propagation, he gives his name to the model of surface waves known as Love Waves.

Sedleian Professor of Natural Philosophy at Oxford University from 1899 until his death in 1940, he was the author of seminal works including the two-volume *A Treatise on the Mathematical Theory of Elasticity*, while his many honours and awards include the Royal Society Royal Medal and the London Mathematical Society De Morgan Medal.

Taking to the heavens, **Stanley G. Love** is the American scientist and NASA astronaut born in Oregon in 1965.

Joining the space agency in 1998, he has been involved in a number of Space Shuttle missions and also, in 2012, the NEEMO 16 undersea exploration of the ocean depths from the DeepWorker 2000 submersible.

One bearer of the Love name with a particularly unusual claim to creative fame was the American puppet maker, puppeteer, costume designer and actor **Kermit Love**.

Born in 1916 in Spring Lake, New Jersey, he is best known as a designer and builder for *The Muppet*

Show and also characters for *Sesame Street* including Big Bird, Cookie Monster and Oscar the Grouch.

It is only by coincidence, meanwhile, that the Muppet character Kermit the Frog shares his surname – having met puppeteer Jim Henson some five years after he created it.

Having also worked on Broadway and for American Ballet, he designed costumes for a number of noted productions including the 1943 musicals *One Touch of Venus* and *The Wind Remains* and the 1944 ballet *Fancy Free*.

For the 1965 ballet *Don Quixote*, he memorably created, along with other stunning items, a 28ft (8.5m) marionette giant.

Having also portrayed the character of Willy the hot dog vendor, on *Sesame Street*, he died in 2008, aged 92.